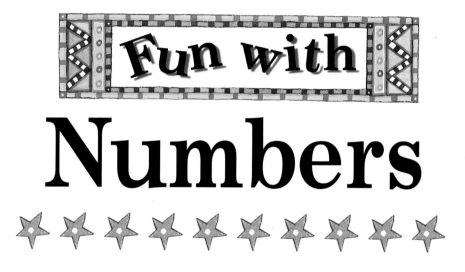

Numbers

THE MILLBROOK PRESS
Brookfield, Connecticut

Published in the United States in 1998 by

M

The Millbrook Press, Inc.
2 Old New Milford Road
Brookfield, Connecticut 06804

First published in the UK in 1998 by

Belitha Press Limited
London House, Great Eastern Wharf
Parkgate Road, London SW11 4NQ

Series editor: Honor Head
Series designer: Jamie Asher
Illustrator: Brigitte McDonald
U.S. Math Consultant: Henrietta Pesce

Patilla, Peter.
Fun with numbers/written by Peter Patilla; illustrated
by Brigitte McDonald.
p.   cm.
Summary: Presents picture puzzles that help the
reader identify and match numbers from one to ten.
ISBN 0-7613-0957-8 (lib. bdg.)
1. Number concept–Juvenile literature. 2.
Mathematical recreations–Juvenile literature. 3.
Picture puzzles–Juvenile literature. [1. Number
concept. 2. Mathematical recreations. 3. Picture
puzzles.] I. McDonald, Brigitte, ill. II. Title.
QA141.3.P38 1998
513.2'11–dc21
98-16664
CIP AC

Printed in Hong Kong

Fun with

Numbers

written by
Peter Patilla

illustrated by
Brigitte McDonald

About This Series

The four books in this series, *Fun With Numbers, Fun With Shapes, Fun With Sizes,* and *Fun With Patterns,* provide an engaging format to explore beginning mathematical concepts with children. They may investigate the books on their own, but extending this investigation with an adult will bring added value to the experience. The following suggestions are provided as a guide for you to help your child or students get the most from the series.

Fun With Numbers

Children naturally develop number sense by having daily experiences with numbers. For example, they know they are 5 years old, that they have 5 fingers on each hand, and that 5 cookies are more of a treat than 2. All of these examples explore number sense: the idea of 5, the concrete representation of 5, and the quantity of 5. Using manipulatives, ask, "Would 5 cookies be enough to give 6 children a snack?" This will allow children to explore quantitiy as well as making critical decisions using number sense. In this book, children are presented with puzzles and games that give them opportunities to count, as well as strengthen pictorial and symbolic numerical understanding.

Before opening *Fun With Numbers*, talk about how children use numbers every day. Why is it important to know your house number or emergency phone numbers? What other numbers are important? Talk about what it would be like if there were no numbers. How would it affect everyday life? Look at the cover of the book and the numbers on it. Ask the children if there are more sailboats than fish. Make up addition and subtraction problems using the sailboats. As you explore the puzzles and games in *Fun With Numbers*, use these ideas to add to the mathematical journey you are about to begin.

A Step Beyond

After you have finished exploring the book, go beyond these pages. Invite children to create a "Numbers About Me" poster. Have them design and color a poster that tells all about themselves, using as many numbers as they can think of. Such numbers can include age, height, family members, address, phone number, and grade in school. When they have finished, hang the poster. As time goes by, make changes as necessary. Don't put the book away—children will want to open *Fun With Numbers* again and again.

Spot the Bug

Find the bugs with...

two patches

three spots

four patches

five spots

7

Feed the Birds

Match the feeders below to the groups of birds. There should be a nut for each bird in the group.

8

9

Run Rabbit Run

Help the blue rabbit through
the maze to meet the red rabbit.

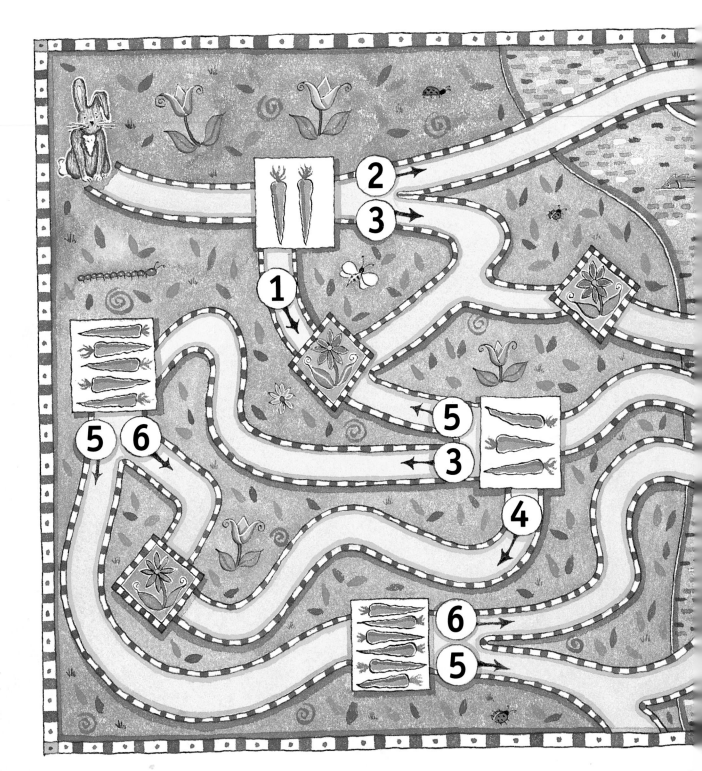

Count the carrots in each square, then follow
the number sign. If you take the wrong path,
you will end up in a flower bed. Go back to
the carrot square and count again.

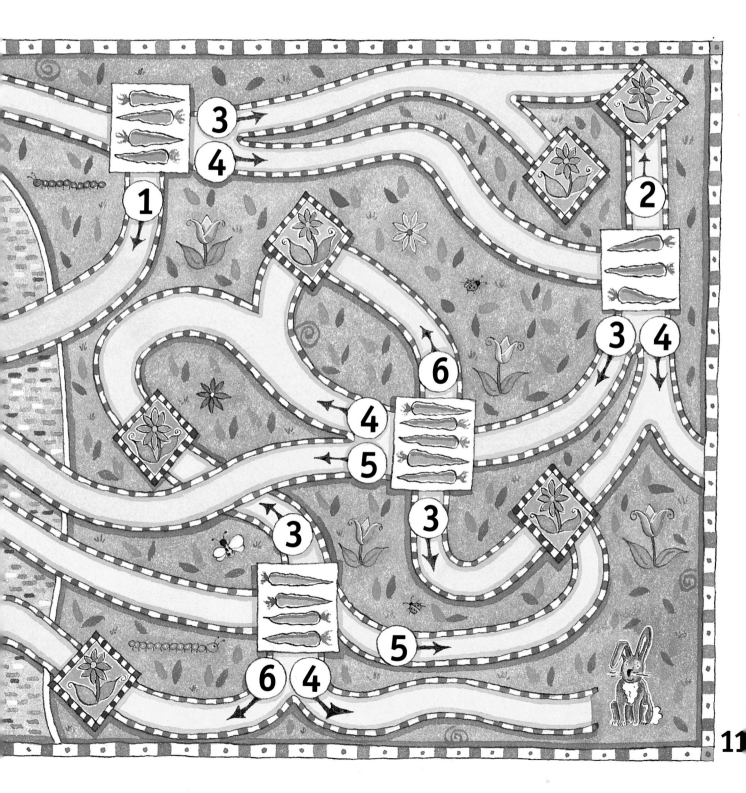

In the Mail

Match the pictures on the cards
to the numbers on the envelopes.

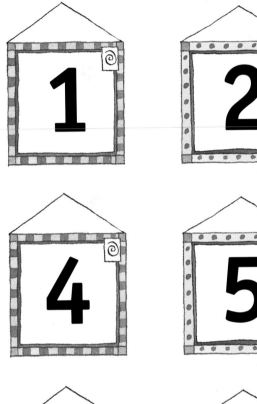

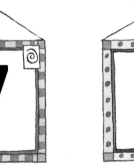

Find the Fruit

Find the apples with...

six holes   eight holes

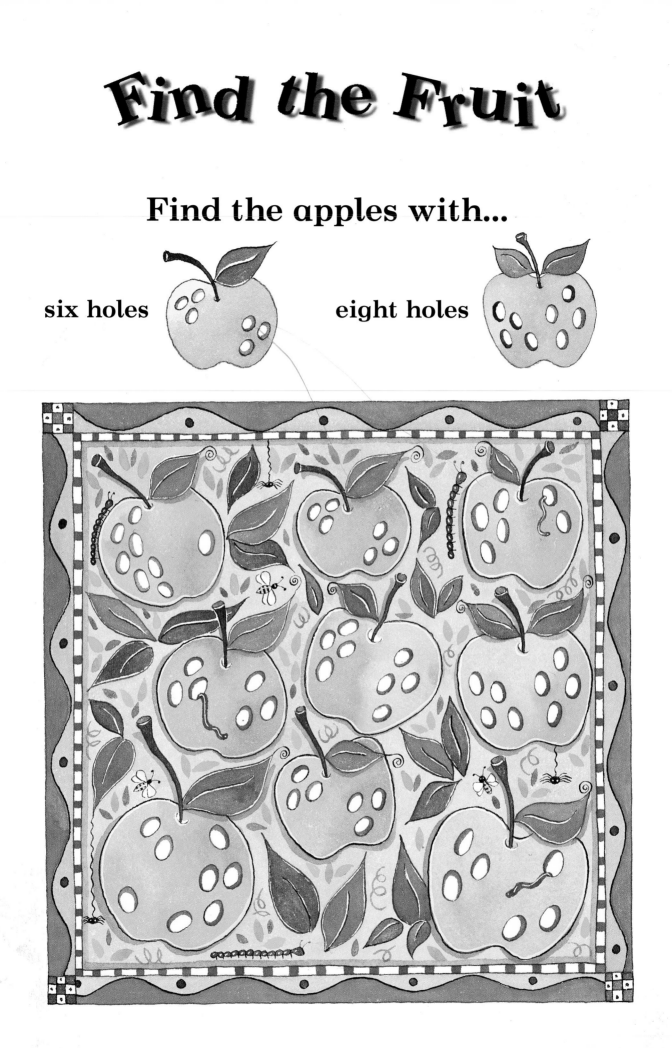

Find the bunches with...

seven grapes

nine grapes

Picnic Party

Look for these in the picture...

one drink

two slices of pizza

three sandwiches

four bananas

five burgers

six oranges

seven strawberries

eight pieces of cake

nine cookies

ten cherries

Number Search

Find these numbers
hiding in the pictures...

0   1   2   3   4

5   6   7   8   9

Clothesline

Match the buttons below
to the shirts on the line...

one button

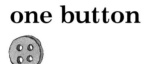

two buttons

three buttons

four buttons

five buttons

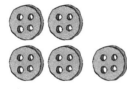

six buttons

seven buttons

eight buttons

nine buttons

ten buttons

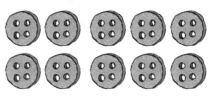

Toy Cupboard

How many of these toys can you see on the shelves?

green balls

brown bears

blue boats

pink buckets

orange bricks

23

Snail Trails

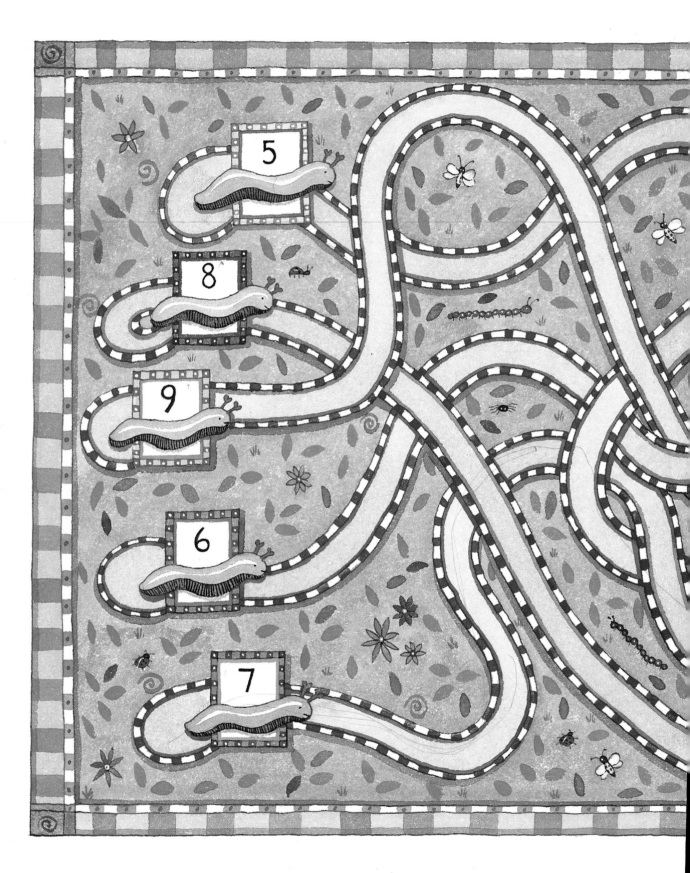

Follow the trails to find the home that belongs to each snail.

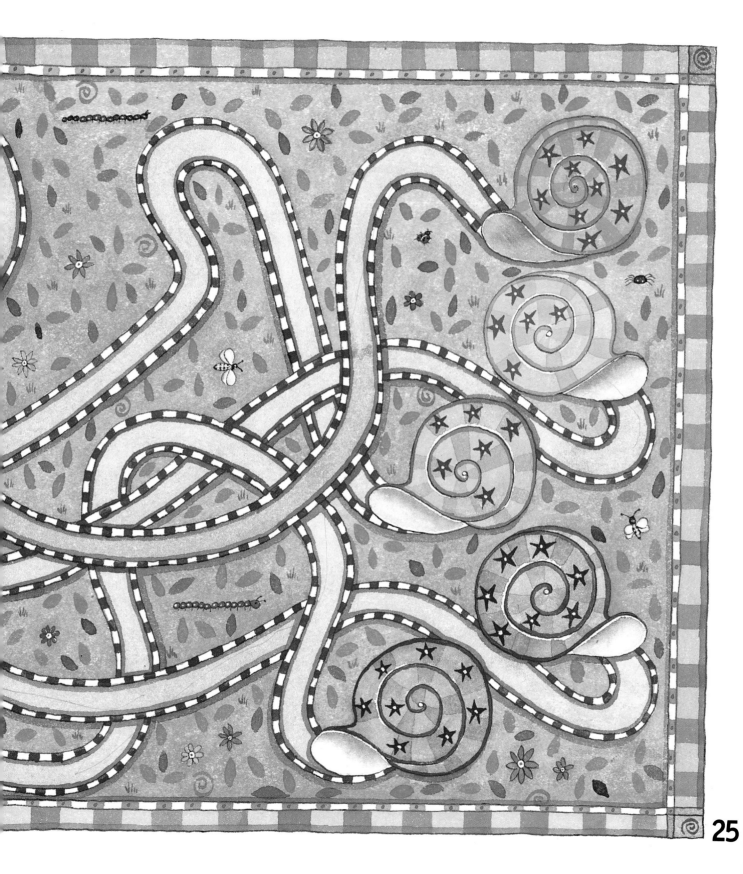

Match the Cards

How many sets of cards can you find?
There is a picture card, a number card,
and a star card in each set.

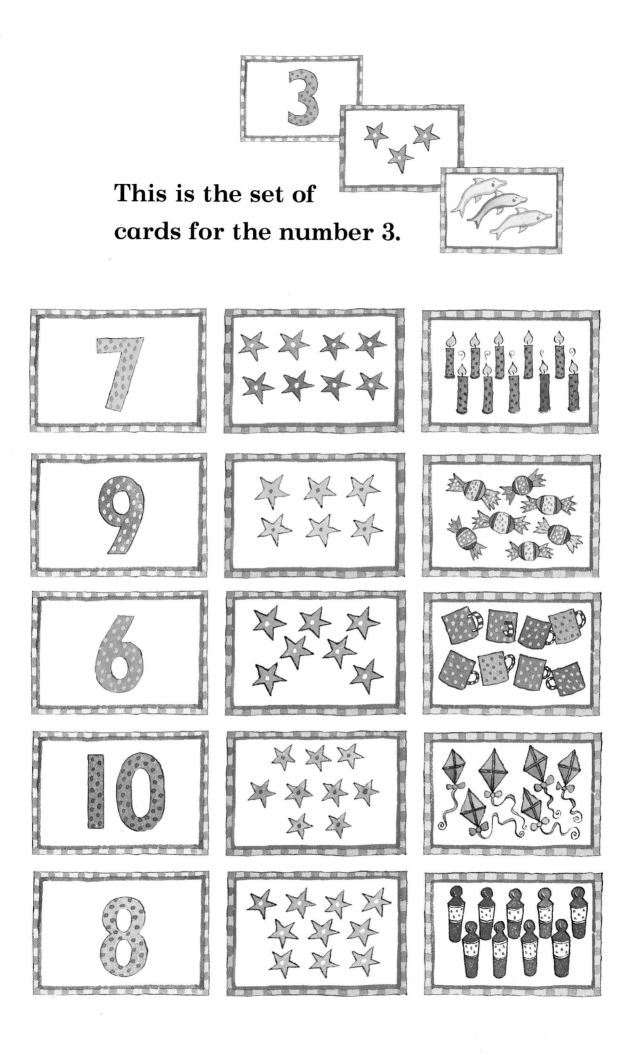

This is the set of cards for the number 3.

Number Train

Each car should have ten sacks.
Find the ones that don't.

Flower Paths

Find a path through the maze by collecting the flowers in number order from 1 to 10.

Numbers

0 zero

1 one ⭐

2 two ⭐ ⭐

3 three ⭐ ⭐ ⭐

4 four ⭐ ⭐ ⭐ ⭐

5 five ⭐ ⭐ ⭐ ⭐ ⭐

6 six ⭐ ⭐ ⭐ ⭐ ⭐ ⭐

7 seven ⭐ ⭐ ⭐ ⭐ ⭐ ⭐ ⭐

8 eight ⭐ ⭐ ⭐ ⭐ ⭐ ⭐ ⭐ ⭐

9 nine ⭐ ⭐ ⭐ ⭐ ⭐ ⭐ ⭐ ⭐ ⭐

10 ten ⭐ ⭐ ⭐ ⭐ ⭐ ⭐ ⭐ ⭐ ⭐ ⭐